Highly Sensitive

Book Bundle:

Highly Sensitive People Going Strong

&

Love And Relationship As A Highly Sensitive Person

Josephine T. Lewis

Contents

Highly Sensitive People Going Strong

A guide on understanding yourself as a highly sensitive person and how to turn your traits into strengths when dealing with other people

Josephine T. Lewis

Contents

INTRODUCTION

An estimated 1 in 5 Americans currently lives with Sensory-Processing Sensitivity according to Elaine Aron, PhD, a foremost authority on the subject, placing millions in a category better known as Highly Sensitive Persons; HSP's. That estimates to be nearly 15-20% of the population. Though this percentage rivals that of anxiety disorders, few truly understand what being an HSP entails or how to live with the personality trait. Increasing awareness and offering insight into the lives of HSP's can help generate a greater understanding of the matter and what it takes to find joy in this trait rather than letting it overcome you.

Though many misguided people, view being an HSP as a weakness, the opposite is actually true. Feeling everything to a greater extreme than most could certainly alter the way you live your life, but the impact doesn't need to be a negative one. This book digs deeper into exactly what it means to be an HSP as well as ways of controlling how the world affects you. Once you're equipped with a better understanding of yourself and how this personality trait functions, you'll be able to harness the power of this trait and use it to your advantage as well as that of others.

CHAPTER ONE: COMMON MISCONCEPTIONS

Before delving into the intricacies of HSP's, it's important to debunk the most common myths surrounding them. Contrary to popular belief, heightened sensitivity doesn't equate to emotional weakness. It's actually an inherent physical trait. Being an HSP means you're more aware of certain elements of the world around you; therefore, you're affected by these factors more profoundly than other people.

Although being an HSP could be confused with an anxiety disorder, some of the physical effects of being an HSP can generate some natural anxiety. We will go into more of that issue in this book and how to limit intensities of anxiety and efforts to suppress anxiety associated with heightened senses as well. Generalized anxiety disorder, panic disorder, and social anxiety disorder are the three main anxiety disorders that uneducated people of the matter, can confuse with, or assume as, hypersensitivity or someone who is an HSP. All of these anxiety disorders have some similar characteristics to being highly sensitive that could lead someone to think that it is all the same. A generalized anxiety disorder can produce irritability in a person. Irritability is prone to occurring in an HSP from over-stimuli to their surroundings. Panic disorder causes an individual to avoid places where previous panic attacks have happened. Social anxiety disorder causes an individual to avoid places where large crowds will be. When an HSP is susceptible to noises, sights, and sounds, they start to have a good idea of what places their senses can or cannot tolerate. The difference between an HSP and someone with anxiety is that an HSP is motivated to avoid conflict with their senses, while an individual with anxiety is motivated by fear that their anxiety or a panic attack will strike.

Not to be confused with hypersensitivity, this doesn't necessarily mean you're apt to easily get your feelings hurt by the seemingly harmless actions of others. Friends, loved ones and coworkers needn't walk on eggshells around you in an effort to prevent an unavoidable emotional breakdown. You will, however, notice subtleties in their behavior even when they attempt to keep them hidden. Hypersensitive is defined as "abnormally or excessively sensitive, either psychologically or in physical response". It's easy to see why some people could confuse this as the same thing as being "highly sensitive". Highly sensitive, however, is defined as "Sensory processing sensitivity, has been described as having hypersensitivity to external stimuli, a greater depth of cognitive processing, and high emotional reactivity". Even though hypersensitivity is in the definition of what it means to be "highly sensitive", they are still completely different. The word hypersensitivity in the definition is referring to "external stimuli". When a truly hypersensitive person experiences hypersensitivity, it is due to internal stimuli.

On another note, being an HSP isn't indicative of being shy or introverted. You notice far more details than other people, so you're up against processing more sensory input than most of those could imagine. If you've ever tried to discuss all those extra nuances with others, you probably have firsthand knowledge of their lack of understanding as well as their utter inability to offer any helpful insight. As a result, you look inward for answers; in turn, this leads others to believe you're shy and introverted.

Chapter Two: What Does it Mean to be Highly Sensitive?

As alluded to earlier, being highly sensitive means you're more in tune with, and easily impacted by, stimuli you'll encounter on a regular basis. Some HSP's are only perceptive of a few environmental aspects whereas others experience the full scope of possibilities. It's different for everyone, but some of the common elements include:

Sound

Plenty of people seem more than capable of simply tuning out the "background noise" of life. They're unaffected by the low drone of the television at a restaurant, the slightly louder din of music coming from speakers overhead, large groups of diners growing gradually louder in an attempt to hear one another over all the other racket and the one person seated at the table next to them practically screaming details of his or her personal life to someone over the phone. You probably don't fall into this category.

Even one of those previously-mentioned layers of commotion is enough to grate on your nerves like the shriek of a dentist's drill. When combined, the cacophony can be maddening. Particularly rambunctious work settings, crowded restaurants and any other types of mass chaos at high volumes aren't the best environments for you.

While many might see this as a significant lifestyle impediment, it could also be considered an advantage with which few people are gifted. A dull, barely perceptible thud from under the hood of a vehicle would go unnoticed by most, but for you, it's an immediately obvious sign your car slung a belt. You know long before anyone else in your home the fridge is on the verge of breaking down just by the slight change in its typical dull roar.

Smells

Humans are among many species found to be profoundly affected by the olfactory senses. No matter how vivid, beautiful or neatly arranged something may be, if it smells bad, we don't want any part of it. As a highly sensitive person, this may be especially true for you.

Perhaps traffic on the interstate comes to a standstill. Other drivers are talking amongst themselves or standing by their vehicles craning their necks to find out what the holdup might be. You, and any other HSP's caught up in the event, know it's a fatal accident without even needing to ask. You're on the verge of dry heaving from the combination of exhaust fumes and the odor of death wafting from the scene.

Others may notice and comment on that ever-present person in line at the supermarket wearing far too much perfume or cologne, but it could be enough to physically trigger an asthma attack for an HSP. Stale cigarette smoke or the odor of moth balls lingering on a winter coat is more than a mild annoyance for you. HSP's are the first to know when baby's diaper needs changing or someone accidentally leaves a candle burning on the edge of the bathtub.

Foods and Beverages

This aspect can be approached from a couple different angles. If you're affected by sounds and smells, you're also likely to be more sensitive to certain tastes or their prominence. HSP's may have a higher-than-average aversion to sour candies. What causes mild temporary lockjaw for most may bring about intense pain for you. Your friends may be munching happily away on the spiciest Thai food available at local establishment; meanwhile, a meal ranking low on the heat scale leaves you sweating, in tears and feeling blindly around the table for the first drink you find.

Spice, sweetness and tartness could certainly limit your menu options, but HSP's are also more prone to the effects of specific substances. Caffeine would be a prime example. A single soda or cup of coffee may be enough to bring about jitteriness, heart palpitations and irritability.

You're likely to be more susceptible to the effects of alcohol, too. The same could be said of some medications. Prescription pain killers incapable of taking the edge off for most people might leave you passed out in a matter of minutes only to wake up an hour later experiencing intense nausea.

Light

Sight is another of the sensory perceptions affected by high levels of sensitivity. You may find yourself in need of sunglasses even on overcast days. The 40-watt bulb in the lamp across the room could seem blinding to you at certain angles. Fluorescent lighting working in unison with skylights in your typical department store could bring on skull-splitting headaches, and passing by a vehicle sporting LED headlights on a dark night may be a literal hazard in your case.

Pain

A number of HSP's also experience low tolerances for pain. What others would describe as mild discomfort could render you inoperable. If you're one of the many who's extraordinarily susceptible to pain medication, there may be little you can do to combat this issue.

On the other hand, this could also be a blessing in disguise. Your heightened awareness gives you greater insight into certain types of pain. Those able to withstand higher levels of pain actually tend to place themselves at greater risk. Being unable to tolerate pain makes you more likely to take immediate action when something isn't right whereas others might push their limits to dangerous levels.

Violence

Society has grown numb to violence; after all, we're bombarded with it every day courtesy of the countless media outlets now available. Though others may live their lives largely unfazed by acts of malice, you can't ignore them. Whether fictional scenarios in books, movies and television shows or harsh realities straight from the world's latest breaking headlines, these abominations reduce you to tears. They'll alter your outlook on life and the people around you.

Other People's Emotions

Just as you're the first person in a room to notice the smell of smoke or hear someone's car alarm chirping outside, you're often the only one to pick up on other people's moods and attitudes. You easily realize when someone in the crowd suddenly becomes uncomfortable. You sense a heated discussion across the room well out of earshot when everyone else is oblivious.

Being in tune with the feelings of others also means you're quick to respond. You're the one who wants to help resolve conflicts to keep negativity at a minimum. When you tell someone he or she "sounded angry" in an email or text, you honestly, and most of the time accurately, plucked some subtle clue from the content about which most people wouldn't have thought twice about.

Plenty of HSP's out there make great psychologists, counselors, and educators for this very reason. They process others' tones and body language incredibly well to the point where it is hard for others to hide things from them. Being able to clearly sense that something is going on in someone can give HSP's the upper hand in reading someone like an open book when they may be trying to keep themselves closed off to others. This also makes HSP's great parents as well. On top of all the responsibilities that children bring, this also gives HSP's an advantage to life's challenges. Whether it's trying to tell if a child is being truthful, or if your teenager is battling depression, HSP's will sense it before most other people.

Although being an HSP doesn't speak to a lack of emotional strength on your part, it does leave you more vulnerable to the impact of other people's feelings. Because you notice these more readily than most, they're going to affect you more deeply. In some cases, your drive to keep everyone happy is as much a matter of soothing your own nerves as it is a selfless act, and rightfully so.

Your Own Emotions

You feel everything more deeply than others. You sense tension in a room, and you immediately take it to heart. You're the problem solver, the mediator and, in all likelihood, the only one present who even notices all the problems developing around you. You're quite literally carrying the weight of the world on your shoulders, and you've probably got no one to help share the load.

On top of all that, you're dealing with the sights, sounds and smells to which you're overly vulnerable. In addition to processing all the emotions coming at you and determining how to proceed, you're trying to filter out all the physical elements overloading your senses. It's a lot to process on a regular basis, and it leaves you more susceptible to the emotions you're feeling in your own right.

High sensitivity stems from your nervous system, particularly the reticular activating system; the RAS. This is a tiny bundle of nerves responsible for controlling sensory perception. It sends information to your brain and tells you how to process all those little tidbits. Though the RAS is designed to prevent us from receiving more information than we can take at any given time, it tends to push the boundaries in HSP's.

You may be impacted by all the common stimuli or only a few; at the same time, HSP's are affected by these factors to varying extents. Many of these elements also have deeper implications. Regardless, the effects of this inborn trait are going to filter into every aspect of your life.

CHAPTER THREE: THE UPSIDE TO BEING HIGHLY SENSITIVE

Although there are many obstacles that could get in the way of your senses, there are far too many other traits that serve as a huge plus to being highly sensitive. This is where HSP's have more power than the average person's senses.

Creativity

When your senses are always on overdrive, this brings in a tremendous amount of information that your mind processes differently than most others. You may find a different outlook on a situation that could turn into a brilliant idea for a painting or book. You feel everything much more deeply to levels that give you more emotions that you feel compelled to write about and sometimes to just get off your chest. Many HSP's have occupations as writers and artists for this very reason. The urge to express yourself can be a priority at times. Maybe there's a problem at work and none of your co-workers are coming up with any ideas on how to solve the matter. You, however, will be one of the firsts to suggest a solution and your idea is more likely to work since you have to brain power to already have thoroughly thought everything out.

Health

There are some traits that come with being an HSP that could benefit health. HSP's are likely to have faster reflexes, keeping them out of harm's way. HSP's are also less likely to use stimulants like coffee. It is easier to wake up when your senses seem to always be awake. The long term effects of coffee could range from Irritable Bowel Syndrome (IBS), complicating pre-existing diabetes, and can increase the risk of heart disease especially when coffee is unfiltered. Since you are the first to notice subtle changes in the world around you, you will also be able to spot when some changes occur in your body or your normal routine. HSP's are highly in tune with their bodies. This serves you the upper hand in noticing anything that could be a sign of something serious that could turn into a more potentially life-threatening or a life-altering situation. Symptoms and outcomes could turn for worse without being spotted early on with your quick and thorough senses.

Sense of Self

When you notice a hundred more details than a few, you have more chances of having a thorough knowledge of who you are and what you truly desire in life. This allows HSP's to figure out their desired road map to life much more quickly than most others. While the average person may be stumbling around from career to career, and still wondering what they are chasing, HSP's are already on the run for their life goals. Determination is easier found when you desire a goal ten times more than others with the same goal and average senses. Every positive and negative reaction HSP's face in life is only an intense indication of who they are or what their bodies can't withstand.

Sense of Pleasure

When HSP's find a new favorite song, movie, or hobby, they have a more intense experience with these new discoveries. This could be linked to higher dopamine levels in the brain. Dopamine is released from neurons in the brain whenever we reach a goal and helps give us motivation to reach our goals and the things we want most. This is another key in the lives of HSP's. You know what you love and you have motivation and determination to achieve goals. Whether you love art, love doing a great job at work, or have a big dream that you strive to make reality, your heightened sense of pleasure will help push you through. Having a better understanding of yourself only makes it crystal clear what you love and what goal you are working towards.

Vivid and Emotional Dreams

HSP's are not only more likely to have intense vivid dreams that pertain to emotional areas of their life, but they are much more likely to recall many details about their dreams. Dreams are a very inner reflection of our lives and subconscious. There are dream dictionaries online that can be used to translate the specific meaning of objects and colors that appear in dreams. When HSP's pay close attention to these indications of what their subconscious is speaking, it could help them realize things that they are missing in their waking life.

Compassion and Kindness

When HSP's have a higher sense of what they feel and who they are, they also have a better sense of what other people feel and who they really are. This is another reason why they make good counselors and teachers. HSP's are more likely to have a big heart and a good understanding of what can potentially hurt others. This allows them to give out kindness more freely and feel a deep level of compassion for others.

Intuition

Not claiming that HSP's are psychic, but that details that most people are likely to overlook, can add up easier in the mind of an HSP. This allows you to predict how things will play out in the near future. HSP's have a great sense of situations and are able to feel energy. You are the first to point out that something isn't right in a situation. Your gut instincts can drive you through situations that most people have no second thought about. Instead of thinking of yourself as an HSP with five heightened senses, it's as if you have six senses.

Sense of Nature

HSP's have also been known to easily predict weather. You are the first to notice the change in the wind and humidity levels. Sometimes, you are just able to sense when a storm is coming. HSP's also feel more pleasure from being around nature. You are more likely to be influenced and calmed by a plant or water fountain in your house or workspace. When you go camping or on a brief walk, you will get more out of the experience. Your friends that may join you won't notice the way moss grows on various objects, or the way the birds change their chirping tones. The leaves rustling against each other in the wind will send your senses into an inner pool of peace.

Hard Workers

Since HSP's are more likely to have high levels of motivation and be very determined individuals, it makes complete sense for them to be dedicated, hard workers. They are prone to also be perfectionists. When you notice so many details at once in a project, you may have the compelling desire to address every odd and end that pops out at you. Although some employers may become irritated by this nature, other employers out there love people who are this hard working and take the time to thoroughly complete their tasks and assignments. Along with HSP's having great gut instincts, fast reflexes, and better memories for either dreams or a real life occurrence, there's no question why some of them also make great detectives. While observing details and being able to quickly recall them, they will also notice when someone's tone of voice or body language indicates that they are lying. Although some HSP's cannot handle the gruesome reality of criminals and cases, some of them seem to be made for the job. Any person that processes and completes a task thoroughly does a diligent job. The diligence is ten times more when you are an HSP.

CHAPTER FOUR: HOW TO LIVE WITH HIGH SENSITIVITY

Being so intensely influenced by the environment has a way of making life difficult. Becoming a hermit and pushing away the outside world may seem tempting, but it's not the answer. Keep in mind, even at home, the incessant ticking of an analog clock or your children tapping their pencils on their half-finished homework is going to work its way into the very depths of your mind. That being said, you can take a number of measures to help block the negative influences.

Headphones

Noise cancelling headphones could be your best friend if you're an HSP. They'll minimize the cacophony taking place around you and allow you to more easily process what's inside your head. Alternatively, you might consider a simple pair of ear buds. You'll have the freedom to choose the sounds you hear and control their volume.

Alternatives to Conventional Medication

Being more susceptible to pain as well as the medications meant to alleviate it could lead to a fair amount of misery, but your heightened sensitivity to substances may mean you don't need the same medications your peers take for discomfort.

Children's acetaminophen, Ibuprofen or even cold and cough remedies might be enough to help. Steam and Neti pots could be suitable solutions for sinus congestion. Hot and cold compresses are also simple and effective options for a range of less complicated issues.

Lower the Lights

Whenever possible, close the blinds or curtains to block out natural light, and keep artificial illumination turned low. Sunglasses are an obvious countermeasure for the outdoors, but don't be afraid to rely on them inside as well. Having random strangers give you odd glances and tap their temples to let you know you "forgot" to take off your shades is a small price to pay for fewer and less intense headaches and eye pain.

Small Avoidances

You can't avoid everything negative in life, but there's no shame in just saying "No" at times. Tell those in your social circle that you have no desire to see the latest blockbuster blood bath. Don't watch the news; quickly scroll past any social media posts depicting violence, crime or hateful activities. If anyone wants to discuss "what happened the other day", gently explain you can't talk about it. It's okay to perpetually remain behind the times, especially if you're happier and healthier as a result. Another thing you can do is focus on finding certain places and specific times that suit your need for less commotion just to get errands done. For instance, go to a grocery store that has a lesser amount of customer flow either most of the time or some of the time. Keep an eye out for when most times throughout the day that will be busier. After five on the weekdays whenever most people are getting off work, and weekend evenings when most people will be out are times that you should keep in mind to prepare yourself for the flock of chaos that your sense might endure. Finding those small windows for productive times can make a great difference for the things you can't avoid or put off.

Walk Away

Little can be done to dodge overpowering smells aside from nose plugs, and they're not very practical. Oddly enough, smell is the one sensory perception not sent through the body's natural sensory filtration system; the RAS, before reaching the brain. Still, the high sensitivity trait is hardwired into the brain as well as the entire nervous system. If the situation allows, no harm is likely to come from walking away or politely excusing yourself. The same can be said of scenarios where the volume exceeds your limits or negative feelings radiating from others have you on edge. Always be realistic with yourself and never minimize the overwhelming stimuli that can constantly come in. Take yourself out of the equation when necessary.

Seize Opportunities

While shutting out the entire world is neither healthy nor possible in most cases, a certain amount of seclusion is recommended. As an HSP, you need time for yourself and a quiet place in which to enjoy it. Forgo parties you know will be too boisterous for your own comfort. If working at home is an option, jump at the chance. You'll have far more control over your work environment in your own home, and conflicts between coworkers aren't likely to affect you quite so severely. Do some of your shopping online from home when the local malls and outlet centers are sure to be crowded and over-lit.

These are general resolutions relevant to everyday scenarios. As you delve into specific areas of your life, more in-depth solutions come into play. You can't control all the situations you'll encounter at home, at work or in a social setting, but you certainly have the power to decide how they're allowed to affect you.

Home Life

Take pride in your home and make it a place that is relaxing to come home to and decompress. Your senses could have you feeling on edge from your day at work or errands that forced you to run around into crazy environments. While you can't control the world or the chaos of certain places, you can always make efforts to turn your home into an environment that gives your senses some relief. If the sight of clutter or too many wall decorations is too much for your senses to handle, take a day to de-clutter and simplify your décor. Perhaps your home is bare and has barely any feel when you come home. Don't let the constant demands of life away from home distract you from spending time on little things that could make a great difference every time you walk in your front door. Put peace in your home so it can return the favor to you.

Acceptance

As easy as it sounds, it can be hard for some people with high sensitivity to accept their trait. It can be tough for friends and family members to also accept especially if they are tired of having to go to certain restaurants, or save their violent movies to be watched with other people more tolerant of those genres. When an HSP picks up on this irritability that some of their loved ones face, they try to ignore their problems and pick activities or places to go to that are too much for their senses to handle. Understanding how easily senses can be triggered can cause an HSP to become very indecisive or possess the need for control over a situation. Although you can't control the world around you, there are ways to cope with the many obstacles you could be faced with. Remember to always be realistic with yourself and what your senses are able to endure. This acceptance can always help you avoid situations that could make you look bad. When you inevitably have get up and leave, or remain detached from the situation by limiting conversation and social interaction by putting in ear plugs, this could give off a negative impression to those around you. That is never a good look. When you have those gatherings that you can't get out of and are more than necessary, there are coping skills to help with the over stimuli and some anxiety that can come with it.

Deep Breaths

When you feel that you've come to the point that you need to get up and leave or you want to shut out others in attempt to limit what your senses focus on, focus on taking deep breaths in at a slow pace. This will help calm you down and make you a little more capable of cooperation. Make sure not to breathe in and out at a fast pace as this could make your situation worse by hyperventilating; thus, furthermore stressing you out.

Counting to Ten

When someone says something to set you off, avoid a confrontation or fight by counting to five, ten, or even twenty seconds. Take time to pause and compose yourself before making matters worse that could send your senses off the deep end. HSP's are usually quick to respond to any situation especially if it's a heated argument.

Keep a Positive Sense of Humor

Instead of letting some things set you off or cause you to be increasingly more irritable to the situation, try to stay positive and keep your thoughts from becoming negative. At the very least, try to find humor in a situation before jumping out of your seat or jamming ear plugs in as an attempt to handle the situation. Although, this response might not be appropriate for all occasions. When it's a serious matter at hand, or there is nothing to be confused with humorous, this attempt might not have the ability to make things appear a little more desirable. At most other times, this could lighten the burden that your heightened senses could bring in some situations.

Focus

Although it may seem ironical for someone to tell an HSP to focus, this could sometimes be the response your senses need to be able to give you more control over them. At first, everything around you does not become background noise naturally, but you can attempt to do this by choosing one thing to focus your attention on. For instance, at a concert or restaurant, when there are people all around you and a range of different noises going on, find your focal point. At a dinner, find someone nearby that you can engage in one on one conversation with. Direct your senses towards their responses and reactions to you. This person will have your undivided attention and that will certainly give you a good impression. At a concert, while being surrounded by very enthusiastic fans that can cause your senses irritability, ear plugs obviously aren't the answer. Either focus your eyes on the view of the music artists, or try closing your eyes in an attempt to hear the music better. Although you can't just ignore what your senses pick up on, you can try to direct them in an attempt to distract them from everything you don't wish to focus on and overwhelm yourself with.

CHAPTER FIVE: SOCIAL INTERACTION AS A HIGHLY SENSITIVE PERSON

First and foremost, the importance of explaining your plight to your closest friends and family members can't be overemphasized. There are plenty of others out there who understand very well everything that you struggle with. You may find a couple of your friends are a fellow HSP's and were reluctant to share this with you due to the common stereotypes and misunderstandings. There are plenty of support groups online where you can meet other HSP's that share your struggles and strengths. This can be a good source of help when you need someone to vent to or socialize with and you need someone who understands how challenging it can be. By looking for people that also have this trait, you can limit the amount of negative reactions you face from your social circle. Some will readily attempt to understand what you're going through and accommodate your needs. Others won't comprehend your struggle in the least and will make no effort to understand.

Truly understanding what you're going through will be difficult for those on the outside looking in. Many won't hesitate to voice their doubts. You're bound to hear all the typical objections:

- You're just being overly sensitive.

- You're over-thinking this.

- You take everything too personally.

- You wear your heart on your sleeve.

Of course, there's every HSP's personal favorite:

- Just stop thinking about it.

Few people realize you can't just stop thinking about it. You can't ignore the HSP trait any more than a diabetic can will his or her pancreas to work properly. Anytime you're able to choose the company you keep, try to limit social interaction to those who at least try to understand.

Don't be afraid to tell your friends you can't handle the tastes or aromas of authentic Mexican food. Suggest a more Americanized southwestern-style venue for lunch. HSP's are more likely to have food sensitivities or allergies. Avoid conflict by picking a restaurant with great variety on their menu so you can stick to what works for you while others can be more adventurous with their tastes. Explain just how profoundly a deeply emotional movie will affect you, and ask if a more lighthearted romantic comedy might be an acceptable compromise.

A lot can be said for keeping your go-to social circle small, but in some cases, you'll be faced with larger, less forgiving crowds. Your best friends have their own social lives to live, and they'll have the occasional birthday party or wedding you just can't get out of attending. Family gatherings are also prime examples of potentially nerve wracking events for HSP's. People are excited, they get too loud, lights and music are blaring and any number of smells invade your space. It's enough to send anyone into sensory overload, but you're particularly susceptible.

Being an HSP is by no means a weakness, so play on your strengths. Your unique attention to detail makes you an asset to any event. Focus on the little matters catching your attention. Set right the overturned vases. If the mood in the room seems to be taking a downward turn, tell the DJ to play something with a little more pep. Aunt Sue is obviously unhappy with her current seating arrangements, so direct her to a more comfortable chair. Make a special effort to chat with the attendees everyone else seems to be ignoring, and work your way into the kitchen to get a head start on the cleanup efforts.

Focusing on specific details gives you more control over the situation and directs your attention away from those things apt to bother you. Nonetheless, finding a quieter, less populated room is never a bad idea. Don't hesitate to plan out your escape route, too. Either drive yourself to the venue or have a reliable ride on speed dial, so when you've had all you can take, you can leave just as easily as you arrived.

Caution

In attempt to tune down or tune out your senses, HSP's are more susceptible to abusing drugs and alcohol. While there are some drugs out there that heighten senses, there are plenty of others that can suppress them. Regardless of choice, some HSP's can use these to their own device as a mental wall. Whether they are using it as a way to block out emotions they feel that they cannot deal with, or to suppress emotions in attempt to cope with situations and environments their social circles may take them to, it is something they must monitor. Addictions can arise, thus making life more difficult and damaging to their emotional well-being. Always try to drink moderately and stay away from substances that could have negative impacts on your life.

CHAPTER SIX: BEING A HIGHLY SENSITIVE PERSON ON THE JOB

Workplaces have a tendency to be extremely distracting and unnerving for HSP's. Whereas sharing the complexities of this trait with friends and family members is advisable, coworkers could be considered an exception to the rule. They're likely to confuse high sensitivity with hypersensitivity, and this transposition will make them uncomfortable. When it comes to work, the physical aspects of your personal space are the easiest to address.

Noise cancelling headphones come into play again if falling back on them won't interfere with your job. In the event a lamp from a neighboring desk is too bright, try rearranging your workspace if at all possible. Plenty could be said for a strategically placed plant or picture frame, too.

Your human resources department is at your disposal. They're there to keep employees happy, healthy and productive. Don't be afraid to ask them for help. If your chair hurts your joints or your hard drive makes a repetitive squawking noise, let them know. Approach them from a concentration and productivity point of view, though, rather than crediting your higher-than-average perception.

Moving on to the less superficial and more difficult-to-fix matters, you take criticism to heart more so than other people. It doesn't hurt your feelings, but it does speak to the drive to please people so common to HSP's. Receiving negative feedback could ultimately affect your confidence. If it starts to get to you, make a mental list of all the elements eliciting praise or, as is the case in many workplaces, no comment at all. Incorporate the main point of the criticism into your future efforts but not the negative tone behind it.

Dealing with Stress

Rushed schedules and pending deadlines contribute to your already high stress levels, and the amount of pressure you place on yourself as an HSP only compounds the matter. Work can quickly and easily become overwhelming. Give yourself realistic goals and a realistic time frame to complete tasks. This will limit the amount of unnecessary stress that your senses endure.

Decompression Time

HSP's need more time than average people to decompress. Giving yourself a little time to unwind throughout the day can help keep you calmer. If possible, try to set aside a day in your week to focus on things that are pleasurable to you or to just relax. In some cases, this time may need to be worked into your daily commute or come in the form of a walk during your lunch break. If nothing else, escape to the restroom for a moment to take a few deep breaths and organize your thoughts. Give yourself a designated place to retreat to like an office space or your bedroom. Try taking a hot bath or shower to help tightened muscles relax. An occasional or regular massage is always a great idea. Whether you work at a desk, do construction, or are up on your feet all day for your place of work, certain muscles are targeted to be tighter than others. You may not even realize what muscles are prone or use to being tense, and being an HSP makes your muscles more likely to tighten up in certain areas when you are stressed by your over-active senses. Listening to water sounds or zen music in your spare time is another way to calm down those senses.

More Sleep, Less Coffee

Getting at least eight hours of sleep each night goes a long way toward keeping your stress levels at a minimum. If you're getting less than seven hours of sleep each night, it can contribute to irritability, and lower levels of concentration and productivity. Having your usual cup of coffee in the morning could also contribute to irritability and other negative side effects that have been mentioned. Using coffee to combat the hours of sleep you aren't getting is likely to be a bad combination.

Food for Thought... And Your Senses

As simple as it may sound, a balanced diet will also contribute to maintaining your composure and sanity. Recurring hunger throughout the day can also be another contributing factor to irritability. Eat quality meals and snacks throughout the day that are packed with protein to keep you going. Omega-3 fish oil supplements have also been thought to support cognitive and emotional health. Being well rested and keeping blood sugar regulated have both been proven to help improve focus and concentration. This is monumentally important for HSP's.

A Team Player

In light of your ingrained empathic capabilities, multi-faceted mental approach to the world and the level of thought you put into everything you do, your coworkers would be hard-pressed to find a better team player than you. Though hectic days and time limits may leave you rattled, you'll be the one who jumps in, delegates responsibilities to those most suited for each task and motivates everyone else to persevere.

Chapter Seven: Love and Romance through the Eyes of a Highly Sensitive Person

HSP's long for closeness in a relationship. Love runs more deeply for those with this trait, but so do anger, fear, passion and other emotions. Because romantic partnerships involve greater intimacy and vulnerability than other types of social interaction, the notorious HSP-driven attention to even the seemingly tiniest detail could be the greatest source of conflict in this type of setting.

You probably go out of your way to make your significant other feel loved and appreciated. As far as you're concerned, maintaining a strong connection isn't an option; it's a necessity. With all the time and energy you devote to catering to your partner's every need, you're likely to feel as if you're putting more into the relationship than you're getting in return. In truth, you are.

This doesn't mean your significant other doesn't love or care about you. He or she just doesn't place as much emphasis on anything as you do. In your eyes, failing to text or call at the usual time is an indication your partner is losing interest. From his or her point of view, it's nothing more than a slight oversight. You need validation of your emotions, so you try to make your significant other understand how much that breakdown in communication hurts you. In turn, he or she points out "you're being too sensitive".

Further attempts to drive home your point aren't likely to be progressive. Your significant other will become angry and defensive and may go so far as to mention the potential benefits of psychiatric assistance, which makes you feel even less validated. He or she isn't being as cold hearted as it seems. Again, to your partner, a missed text is just a missed text, and it's no big deal. In an ideal world, understanding and legitimate compromise would be the word of the day for an HSP in a romantic relationship, but it's probably not going to happen. Being an HSP gives you a demand for being better understood. In attempt to better understand each other, try using your senses to put yourself in their shoes and see yourself from their point of view. You may notice things that you yourself, have been blinded to or things you have overlooked on your part while being distracted by the actions of your partner.

Since you readily sense minuscule changes in other people's moods and behaviors, you'll know right away when your significant other is upset about something. Asking what's wrong is a wonderful and straightforward way of letting him or her know you care. Still, it's important to keep in mind, your partner isn't going to talk to you about an issue until he or she is ready to do so.

As is the case with repetitive confrontations over the significance of a call, text or other small gesture, subjecting your partner to further questioning regarding the problem at hand is only going to leave you both frustrated. You'll begin to emotionally pull away from the relationship, and your persistence is bound to push away your partner. Sometimes, you have to just let go and accept your partner's inability to understand why certain elements mean so much to you.

Enjoy the efforts he or she does put into the relationship. Though you're well within your rights to hope to receive the same amount of energy you give, expecting that from someone who's not an HSP is only going to end in disappointment. Accept your partner for whom he or she is, and live with the satisfaction of knowing you're going the extra mile because it's just what you do. Your significant other really does appreciate you even if he or she isn't able to express it in the same way you might want.

Dating a Highly Sensitive Person

Although dating a significant other without this trait may be difficult, there are still other HSP's out there that manage to find one another, and end up falling in love. Elaine Aron, PhD, has even written a book titled, "The Highly Sensitive Person in Love". In the book, she has even included it with self-tests in the beginning, as a device for couples to complete and see how they rank in attempt to help better understand each other. Elaine elaborates that there are two types of people that come with the HSP trait. She states that there are "Sensation Seekers" that happen to be more adventurous and out-going as they are driven by pleasurable activities. Other HSP's can remain content and withdrawn from their surroundings in attempt to cope with their heightened senses. In exception to these two personality traits, complications can arise in a relationship.

While one may be planning a trip to Italy or Spain, the other in the relationship is already turning down the thought of getting on a plane and having little control over the environment that they will face in a busy airport. The adventurous HSP will be more driven by their desired goal enough to push them through any unwanted circumstances they may encounter along the way.

Elaine explains the reason for the two types of trait: "Different genes and brain systems seem to govern the two traits." Meaning that just how someone who is an HSP was never given the choice to have normal or heightened senses, goes the same way for the two types of HSP's. You were never given the choice of which senses would be affected and to what extent they would be heightened.

Although there are complications that come with any relationship, there are other circumstances where two people being an HSP, make them a match made in Heaven. It is said that they are more likely to be happier when paired together for the simple fact that they easily understand each other and to great depths as well. As an HSP, you naturally demand a deeper level of acceptance and love. When your significant other happens to not have the same senses as you, it can be harder to bring them to that deep level of intimacy that you desire to have. When two HSP's find themselves in love and are not pulled away from each other by the two traits there could be, they fall into a deep, rich, inner life of love.

Whether you are dating someone of normal senses, or are dating a fellow HSP that masters a different trait than yours, having heightened senses could ultimately make or break your relationship. It poses for difficulties and complications, and gives various obstacles. You don't get to choose any of your traits, but you certainly know when you are loved when your significant other chooses to love you. Even if he or she can't completely understand the details that you find yourself overthinking at times, your significant other makes you their choice. Being an HSP can be a test or a plus in any relationship.

Chapter Eight: HSP- The Highly Sensitive Parent

Although there are many things to understand as an HSP and how to maneuver your way successfully through life, the one consistent and challenging topic is your life when it comes to your children. Just like all the topics, there are plenty of negatives, but far more positives that make HSP's terrific parents.

HSP's as parents can easily find what makes their child incredibly unique. Although this comes natural to any parent, it is ten times more prevalent in an HSP. When you notice all the things that make your child who they are, you get a good idea of the possibilities and opportunities lined down their path. For this reason, you also have a great sense in knowing what it is that they need to develop and grow into an outstanding adult. Even after that, when they are grown and on their own, you have a great sense of knowing what it is that will help them exceed in life.

Babies

HSP's have their advantages to infants and babies, before they are able to verbally communicate with us. Whether you have become a new parent, or are adding to your family, as an HSP, you will be more in tune with your baby's needs than most others relying on average senses and parental instincts. You are likely to tell right away when your baby has an upset stomach or is developing a cough. This could allow you to get your baby the medical help he or she needs in a faster time frame, preventing or to off-set any negative health effects he or she could face.

Children

Once you become in tune with your baby's needs, you never lose that ability to sense when something is wrong and what he or she needs. By the time that your baby is a child, they have mastered words, walking, and getting in to plenty of stuff. It can be hard for you to discipline your children when you feel their feelings of being upset. The positive side to having to discipline your children when you are an HSP is that you have a better idea of what type of discipline they need to learn from their actions or mistakes. It may still hurt you in the process, as is with every parent. But in order to raise your children to do good, and have less of a need to be disciplined, that's plenty of motivation as parents to make sure they learn from their mistakes and understand why certain repercussions needed to happen.

HSP's as parents also need help in juggling their children's needs in order to juggle their own as well. You are more likely to be irritated, angry, and stressed by the over-stimuli your children can bring you. Whether it's staying over at a friend's house for the night, or taking them to their grandparents for a weekend, or vacation time in summer, any way that you can give yourself a break can go a long way on your behalf. By focusing on each child's unique talents and needs, this can help you find extracurricular activities or hobbies to at least get them out of the house or keep them preoccupied in their room. Try to always keep your cool. As mentioned before, when you feel angry and irritated, you feel it much more passionately. It is not your child's fault that you feel things more intensely. He or she is only focusing on being a kid and doing what kids do. When you lash out at your children, it can negatively affect your relationship with them. Remembering to count to ten can greatly help you avoid losing your cool, better organize your thoughts, and correctly respond to the situation at hand. Take deep breaths to cool down even if you feel that your blood is boiling in your veins.

Raising an HSC- The Highly Sensitive Child

Being an HSP, by now, you will have figured out if you are in fact, raising a "Minnie me". HSC's require more attention and nurturing. It is imperative for them to feel loved and accepted and they strive to please their parents. An HSC that is pleasure driven can be a hassle. They tend to always be in everything and can become easily bored which puts demand on their parents to entertain, preoccupy them, or tolerate their behavior until they move on to the next excitable thing. HSC's also require more care when it comes to discipline. They feel everything much more intensely just as HSP's do. Sometimes moderate efforts could come off more harsh than intended. HSP's will learn to master deciding when it is appropriate to use gentle or harsh punishment, or when to have more or less discussions or explanations for actions that are considered mistakes on their behalf. Again, don't be afraid to ask for help, even if it could come in the form of a family counselor. Whether you include the fact that you are highly sensitive or that your children happen to be also, the counselor should be able to quickly pick up on the misunderstandings each member of the family struggles with. Family counselors are there to help you as a family better understand the needs and wants everyone else, and perhaps, even yourself. Even though HSP's have a better sense of self, that can be mixed up any time one of them takes on the responsibility of raising a little one. All parents naturally put their children's desires in front of their own. While this is extremely important for your children, you also have desires of your own and every child, especially an HSC, desires a happy and healthy parent. Remember to make time for your desires and needs, while also taking care of your children's needs.

Adolescents

When your children grow into adolescents, the problems that seemed difficult when they were younger, start to seem merely simple issues to handle compared to the new challenges you both are faced with when they get to this awkward stage of life. If your child was an HSC, he or she is now an HSA; highly sensitive adolescent. HSA's, mixed with the hormones their body is thriving off of, and the new sense of freedom they are experiencing, is challenging enough. Adolescent's like to totter between the role of a child and the role of an adult. HSP's as parents will also master knowing when they need the stability that children need to keep them calm and collected, or when they need to be treated more like an adult and lectured about their actions and put on the spot. When it comes to their positive and negative behavior, although difficult, those behaviors give you more details than what you had about your child before. Just as it is a huge learning period for your adolescent or HSA, it is another learning experience for you as well. You will have more details to go off of when directing their path that is just starting in life. Perhaps they are still your "Minnie me" and they require more advice from you, as you watch them closely resemble you in your teenage years. You know what mistakes they are prone to, and what is tempting them, especially if they are an HSA.

HSP's make great parents throughout every stage of their children's lives. It is natural for any parent to be hard on themselves, and HSP's can be more susceptible to that self-criticism. As long as you focus on the positive aspects that your child offers, along with their unique talents that can open doors of opportunities for their future, there is little harm that you can do and little failure that can come of it.

CHAPTER NINE: WHAT TO TAKE AWAY FROM THIS

By now, you understand that being an HSP is not weakness at all. It is not hypersensitivity or a disability. It is a trait you are luckily gifted with and gives you strength over most situations if used to your advantage. This does not define you as an introverted or shy person. It could even make you a very out-going person caused by your intense desire to reach your goals and make pleasurable activities possible. You either have some of this trait, or the full spectrum. All five of your heightened senses could very well count as one extra; giving you a total of six. You're able to read yourself and others as an open book. The world you live in is very different from the world everyone else lives in. Being an HSP can sometimes mean you have the creativity to help or enlighten others to perceive it closely to how you do. You have a better shot at living a good and long quality life in the thankfulness of your detection skills and being in tune with what your body is telling you it needs. You never have to second-guess who you are and what you want because your senses readily and thoroughly tell you what you intensely enjoy. You will create exceptional memories throughout life and have the memory to recall most of every one of them. Your compassion towards others makes you an exceptional friend, significant other, and parent. You are prone to being a diligent worker. You are easily a great asset to any employer as you have the determination to tackle all and every detail in a project. Obstacles can sometimes make it difficult to get things accomplished. Be open-minded to other work alternatives and solutions. You can sense obstacles or storms coming from miles away. You will have a higher sense of respect for whatever nature brings when your senses tune in to the natural world around you. There are plenty of complex solutions to the burdens your senses can present you with, but you're likely to come up with a quick, sure-fire way to resolve them. You can be easily determined to find solutions to keep any obstacles from interfering with your quality of life. Never be afraid to say "no", to walk away from a situation, or to seize opportunities no matter how big or small. Your home life has much more to offer than you think when you make it a place that relaxes your senses instead of stimulating them furthermore from your busy day. Never deny what your senses tell you. Never deny that they are heightened. When they seem to overwhelm you, remember to take deep breaths, count to a number before speaking in heated situations, and always keep a positive sense of humor when possible. Focus on the important things when you find yourself in an overwhelming situation. Don't let your senses allow you to overlook a person or the main reason you are there. Don't keep your senses a secret from friends and loved ones and don't be hesitant on bringing fellow HSP's into your own social circle. Be willing to allow for compromise when necessary. Make yourself a useful tool in gatherings of family and friends. Try your best to never turn to drugs and alcohol as an attempt to suppress them or make them more manageable. Addictions will only send your senses into a more extreme type of overdrive. Stress can be inevitable, but it is always manageable. When given the choice, never pack your schedule too full of things to do and too little time to complete them. Always try to allow yourself more time to relax and to sleep. Always pick quality foods to eat instead of unhealthy alternatives. Try to eat more throughout the day to combat hunger that will bring irritability. Love can be difficult for all types of relationships and your heart requires more affection than most. When this seems to be too demanding for your significant other, remember to put your senses in their shoes and evaluate your role in the relationship and things that you may overlook on your part. Try to never minimize your needs and desires as an HSP. Never be afraid to share them with your significant other. When you happen to find yourself in love with another HSP, it could be a match made in Heaven, but don't let your deep levels of intimacy make you naïve to obstacles you both could face. Try not to be unwilling to look for help or advice in attempt to better understand each other. Keep in mind that not all HSP's are designed the same. It is not a disability but a trait. It does not define you, but instead, helps define the undiluted person that you are.

CONCLUSION

It seems HSP's process more sensory input in a single day than most people do in a week. While this gives you a unique view of the world most could never comprehend, it does tend to make life a bit difficult. Understanding this trait you possess and passing your wisdom along to those closest to you, even though they may not fully grasp the concept, are critical to your survival and coexistence with others.

Everyday events like visiting a bustling shopping mall, attending a party or taking the bus to work can be downright excruciating for you, but you're sure to show a level of compassion and consideration for others to which few can compare. Regardless of your level of discomfort, you feel it's your duty to make everyone else feel at home.

At work, as is the case in any other environment, you're an invaluable asset. A drive for excellence and unequalled attention to detail give you an added advantage in all you do. Friends and romantic partners won't find a more loving and empathic person than you with whom to share their lives. They relish every measure you take to show your kindness and affection even if they can't match you gesture-for-gesture.

Though you're better equipped than anyone to make important decisions, you don't want that type of pressure in your life. Whether it's choosing a new brand of laundry detergent or making a life-changing decision on behalf of others, you loathe the possibility of taking the wrong route. Remember, though, if others involved placed the decision solely in your hands, they either had no opinion on the matter or were too afraid to offer their input. Should any backlash arise from your choice, remind the others of these points, don your noise cancelling headphones and make your exit. Remember that you are a great team player, if not, a great team leader at times.

Place as much emphasis on your own health and well-being as you do on other people's. You can't always dim the lights and lower the volume, but seizing opportunities to control elements of your environment when possible will help keep you grounded. When a situation gives you more sensory input than you feel you can handle, focus on your strengths. If all else fails, you have the power to simply remove yourself from the chaos.

Although simple things like headphones and sunglasses can make the world more tolerable, giving yourself extra time to complete certain tasks and securing a quiet place to hide when the need arises will go a long way toward coping with being an HSP. Keep using your empathy and compassion to foster others, but don't expect the same level of contribution from them. They're just not capable of offering it. Through all this, you'll be able to find the same degree of joy you bring to others in your life and prevent the burnouts many HSP's experience without even seeing them coming.

Finally, if you enjoyed this book, then I'd like to ask you for a favor. Would you be kind enough to leave a review for this book on Amazon? It'd be greatly appreciated!

Thank you and good luck!

REFERENCES

- The Highly Sensitive Person:
  http://www.hsperson.com

- 10 Life-Changing Tips for Highly Sensitive People:
  http://www.marcandangel.com/?s=10+Life-Changing+Tips+for+Highly+Sensitive+People

- Tips to Manage Anxiety and Stress:
  https://www.adaa.org/tips-manage-anxiety-and-stress

Thank you!

Thank you for buying *Highly Sensitive People Going Strong*. If you enjoyed reading this book, then I'd like to ask you for a favor, **would you be kind enough to leave a review for this book on Amazon? It'd be greatly appreciated!**

All my best wishes,

Josephine T. Lewis

Highly Sensitive

–

Love And Relationships As A Highly Sensitive Person

Josephine T. Lewis

Contents

Introduction: What does it Mean to be Highly Sensitive?

I want to thank you and congratulate you for buying the book, "*Highly Sensitive: Love and Relationships as a Highly Sensitive Person*".

Some people are under the mistaken impression that they are their thoughts. They truly believe that each event that happens "right" in life is due to properly planning, and everything that goes wrong is their fault. They never stop to think that there is more to them than the constant chatter going on in their minds. You might find yourself getting overwhelmed by strong emotions on a regular basis. This may lead you to think that there is something very wrong with you, and you find yourself constantly stuck on ways to get better or fix yourself.

Maybe you've heard time and time again that you are just too sensitive, or emotional, or intense. After a while of hearing this, you start to believe it. You may not know exactly how you should live, feeling tempted to analyze your life instead of experience it. You might find that when you're alone, you feel much more at ease. Perhaps you feel safer when no one is around; and when you can feel your strong, at times you have inexplicable feelings without having to explain them to others, keeping them under wraps when you are in social situations.

What does it Mean to be Highly Sensitive?

If the above describes you, you are likely a highly sensitive person (an HSP). You may find that you have a hard time trusting your own thoughts or unpredictable emotions and that your sensitivity is often overwhelming or seemingly out of your own control. Being highly sensitive means that you have deeper, stronger reactions to stimuli than other people. This can be anything from a sudden noise, to a disturbing image on television, to emotional content.

Is High Sensitivity a Weakness?

Some may see being sensitive as some form of weakness because it's a type of vulnerability, that it's outside of your conscious control and you also aren't sure what specifically to do with that sensitivity. This leads to judging and suppression of the feelings, making them manifest in weak ways, although this isn't their original state. However, this can actually be a great power if seen in the correct light and wielded the right way.

Love as a Highly Sensitive Person:

True, healthy love is much more likely if you understand this trait in yourself. Many people go through life failing at relationships simply because they haven't recognized a certain trait in themselves. Having a fulfilling relationship with another person is only possible once you fully understand your own traits: how you work, how you think, and how you feel. Only then can you ask another person to accept you and be assertive about what you expect in a relationship.

In this book, you will find out more about what it means to have your specific personality type. You will also discover tips for navigating a relationship either as or with a person who is highly sensitive. Everything does not have to feel like such a struggle. You can have powerful, immediate results from processes that are relatively simple. The better you understand yourself, the more you can thrive in life. Realizing that you are highly sensitive and learning how to embrace rather than struggle against it will open up new doors for you in life.

CHAPTER 1: ARE YOU HIGHLY SENSITIVE?

Sensitivity is the human ability to notice information on a sensory level using our nervous systems. This process is neither good nor bad, but simply neutral. Like a microphone that is sensitive, subtle cues are picked up by the human body and then interpreted with the mind and emotions. Someone with a nervous system that is more sensitive will notice that they can sense the emotions of other people, along with smells, sounds, lighting, and more. That is the essence of what it means to be highly sensitive.

If a human body can be compared to a receiving vessel for stimuli and information, our nervous systems can be compared to the antennae, and highly sensitive people can be said to have highly developed antennae. Knowing and recognizing this trait in yourself is absolutely essential for living fully and having healthy love relationships, but first, you should determine if this personality type fits you.

Questions to Ask yourself to Find out Whether you are an HSP:

There is actually nothing wrong with being this personality type even though it comes with its struggles. We are going to give you some valuable tips on navigating yourself, love, and relationships as a highly sensitive person. But first, here are some questions you can ask yourself to find out whether you fit this personality profile:

- **Do you Tend to Feel Everything?** At times, you feel as though your feelings are tangible and palpable. They can be triggered by just about anything: song lyrics, or even something you read in a book. These instances may be insignificant to others, but to you, they are highly significant, which can be overwhelming at times.

- **Do you Find yourself Scanning the Vibe of Situations?** When you first enter a new place, walk up to a conversation in the middle of it, or meet someone new, you instantly assess and accurately guess what the mood is of that situation? You have the ability to sense when a subject might get emotional or sensitive usually before others do.

- **When something is Off, do you Feel it?** Do you always see through another person's white lie when they tell you everything is okay and it isn't? Do you find it nearly impossible to go along with someone who is acting or putting up a front? If you find yourself experiencing very strong empathy on a regular basis, you are probably highly sensitive.

- **Are you Extremely Polite?** If forgetting to thank someone or say "please" seems unthinkable to you and you nearly always take notice of the manners of others, you are probably highly sensitive. You never want to offend other people and will always go out of your way to be polite, especially to new acquaintances.

- **Do you Love being Alone?** If you have always been fine on your own, rarely ever even feeling lonely, you might be an HSP. There are probably countless ways you can entertain yourself when no one else is around, and being in social situations or working in groups makes you feel like you are on trial. Although you don't always necessarily prefer to be alone, you have never had a problem with it for most of your life.

- **Do you have Mystical Powers of Intuition?** As a highly sensitive person, you take your intuitive feelings seriously and they are nearly always correct. Do you often feel as though you can sense what's happening behind the scenes and obey those feelings? This is a key element in the HSP personality profile.

- **Do you Dislike telling people "No"?** The thought of possibly hurting someone or offending them by saying no is worse to you than actually refusing a favor that someone asks. For this reason, your friends know that you are the one to call when they need someone to count on.

- **Is your Imagination very Powerful?** Do you have extremely vivid dreams and find yourself daydreaming often? Do you find it easy to put yourself into another person's place when they are relating an emotional story to you? An active imagination is a surefire sign of the highly sensitive personality type.

- **Do you Cry Easily?** Emotions are meant to be expressed and tears are only one way to do this. Whether you are happy, anxious, or sad, you tend to cry a lot. This is a good thing! It means you're alive and you should never feel ashamed that you cry often.

- **Do you Tend to Fall in Love Quickly and Intensely?** When people who are highly sensitive fall for someone, it often leads to intense feelings of ecstasy and at times it all happens a bit too fast, leading to anxious fear, overwhelm and a hard time deciphering what is real about the feeling. This can lead to a harder time developing meaningful relationships, staying on the same page, and growing together with a partner.

But don't worry; this book will help you in that area.

- **Are you Particularly Sensitive to Loud Noises?**
  Most people don't enjoy irritating or loud sounds, but
  for you it is nearly unbearable. It makes you want to
  run as far away as you can or stop it however possible,
  especially when it is clashing music. You simply can't
  understand how people don't seem to notice such
  things because they drive you so crazy. You may also
  have a strong adversity to overly bright lights.

- **Have you Struggled with Depression or
  Anxiety?** If you have had difficult experiences in life,
  especially as a kid, you may not feel very safe and find
  that you often feel anxious out of habit. It can be hard
  to deal with such strong emotions and know how to
  handle them correctly. Many highly sensitive people
  feel this way. But don't worry, this book will give you
  some tips for that.

- **Are you Easily Disturbed by Graphic Images?** If
  you are a highly sensitive person, you may find that you
  don't enjoy violence on movies or television the way
  other people do. In fact, you may actively avoid
  watching the news because you are so sensitive to what
  is happening on the screen. You may often wonder how
  people can casually sit and watch such things.

- **Do you take a Long Time to Make a Decision?** You have probably been described as "indecisive" before because you take a while to choose, even with seemingly insignificant decisions. You can't stand the feeling that you made a choice that could have been better, even if it's something like where to eat for dinner. You want your decisions to be the correct ones, every time, leading you to overanalyze situations at times.

- **Are you More Observant than Most People?** You may think of yourself as highly detail-oriented, noticing every small nuance. You could notice that you get overwhelmed easily, especially by natural phenomena. The season changing, a beautiful sunset are enough to take you over or make you feel ecstatic. It's this quality that makes you so good at reading others.

- **Are you Crazy about Animals?** Highly sensitive folks tend to have special bonds with their furry friends, and you may notice if you're an HSP that animals seem to trust and like you instantly. This is because people of this personality type are appreciative of the respect an animal can give unconditionally. While others may see animals as creatures that don't talk, highly sensitive people know better and realize that they are always sending signals with nonverbal communication. Some highly sensitive people may even feel like they relate better to animals than to humans.

If you answered yes to all or even most of these questions, you are definitely a highly sensitive person. Contrary to what you may have always believed about yourself, this is not a weakness at all. The only time it becomes a weakness is when it gets condemned or suppressed. Understanding it fully will give you the key to unlock your great advantages and potential, not just personally, but also in love.

How can you Turn your Sensitivity into Strength?

What you can do, to start off, is become fully aware of the distinction between an emotion and a sensation.

- **Sensations:** Sensations are pieces of sensory data that are completely neutral (such as tightness in your stomach or butterflies). They can be a sudden shot of adrenaline at something unexpected happening or a leap in your chest as a reaction to something.

- **Emotions:** Emotions are a response on a personal level to a sensation that occurs, such as "I am feeling nervous about tomorrow". This has to do with noticing the physical sensation in your body and deciding what it is, giving it a label, such as anxiety, fear, or excitement.

The Issue with Immediately Judging your Sensations:

A problem with sensitivity only arises when we feel sensations and immediately start judging ourselves for them. You can practice learning how to feel whatever sensations are arising in your body in a neutral, interested way. You can start engaging with these sensations as well. You could, for example, notice that your heart is racing and tell yourself that there's nothing wrong with that. This is better than condemning yourself by telling yourself that there is something wrong with you for feeling that sensation.

You are Participating in Life, not just Observing:

It's easy to feel out of control when we imagine that we are watching our lives from the outside. Instead, start envisioning that you are playing the game of life, not just watching from the sidelines. Let yourself become aware of how you feel as a result of whatever situation you find yourself in at the time. You have an advantage of picking up on these subtle energies and you should learn to tune into them instead of ignoring, or worse, criticizing them. Ask yourself what would make you feel better at the moment and then allow the answer to come.

Learning to Trust yourself:

We are smarter than we give ourselves credit for. Your body and its system actually picks up on and knows a lot more than you believe. Start to practice trusting what it tells you. Begin right where you're standing now and take baby steps toward this trust, which takes practice. It is only when we trust ourselves enough that we can have healthy relationships with others, because we can then assert what it is we need, will and will not accept and communicate that to another person. In these ways, you can begin to grow stronger in your connection to yourself.

CHAPTER 2: UNDERSTANDING YOURSELF AS A HSP

Understanding yourself as a HSP is not always the easiest of tasks. People tell you that you're too emotional because you feel things deeper than most people, but there's absolutely nothing bad about being sensitive. Actually, it comes along with its own benefits and challenges, just like any other personality type. There are some people who are highly sensitive that have a tendency toward loneliness due to the fact that others can't always relate to how they feel and think.

How Common is this Trait in People?

It is estimated that about 20 percent of people are highly sensitive, meaning about 1 out of every 5. This quality in a person shows a specific strain of strategy for survival: observing before you act. This means that a HSP's brain works a bit differently than the other 80 percent of humanity.

Biological Differences in Highly Sensitive People:

People who are sensitive don't always get a good rap. Studies show that biological reasons (genes) are actually responsible for these traits. This trait has been studied extensively, even using brain scans (MRIs) to take a look at what makes this type of person different. Research showed that highly sensitive people experience feelings, sounds, and the company of others in a much more intense way than others.

Does Sensitivity Relate to Emotional Intelligence?

EQ, or your emotional intelligence is how good you are at identifying and understanding feelings, both in yourself and other people, and how well you can use this knowledge to effectively navigate your actions and relations with others. Fortunately, people who are highly sensitive do not necessarily have more or less EQ than the average person. HSP feel things a lot more intensely, and these strong feelings may be easier to recognize (potentially leading to beneficial use) than most people. This trait can also help them with communication since they don't only listen to which words another person is speaking but notice subtle cues in both tone and gesture.

The Necessity for Awareness of this Trait in Yourself:

Being aware that you are this type of personality, if you are, is absolutely crucial to you getting the most out of your life. Strong, intense emotions that are not recognized for what they are can have highly negative results and consequences. It's only possible to use emotional intelligence to your benefit as a highly sensitive person if you are aware of your sensitivity. A lot of people go through life struggling because they have yet to realize that they fit this profile and instead wonder what is wrong with them, or why they aren't like others. Becoming aware of this will ensure that you can access the beneficial aspects of their heightened feelings while staying on top of their negative traits.

Qualities to Understand about Yourself as a HSP:

- **You Think Deeper than Most:** You have been described, time and time again, as a deep thinker. Your reaction to sudden, shocking changes is not to charge forward and take control but to retreat back into yourself to think about the situation from every possible angle. Things that seem insignificant to others are very impacting for you. This gives you the ability to see and feel things that others might be blind to, allowing you to express entirely unique perspectives. When you are with the right friend or partner, they will appreciate this trait in you very much, and it will help you flourish.

  If you are not around the right people who understand and appreciate your sensitivity, you may find yourself tempted to ignore social situations or even to turn to drugs or alcohol to numb that intense feelings you have. These can turn into dangerous routes of escape for a highly sensitive person, if they are not careful.

- **You React Strongly to Emotion:** This is something that the average HSP should make sure they are keeping in check: the tendency to react (often without thinking) to what they feel. It's highly possible that these feelings could end up "taking over" and causing you to act in irrational ways. This can cause issues in close relationships, especially if your sensitivity is combined with a tendency toward anxiety.

  Simply learning that you fit the profile of a highly sensitive person is not enough to change this behavior (which may be ingrained). You also have to consciously notice when you are allowing a feeling to take you over and find ways to channel those strong emotions into positive results. This involves knowing how to slow down and label what you are feeing (for example, "I am feeling a bit nervous right now"), and then pause, breathe, and think your reaction through.

- **Criticism can be Hard to Accept for you:** You don't always take criticism very kindly due to your intense reactions and feelings. You may get overly offended and react very strongly when you first receive the words from another, but your strength is that you are more likely to take their words to heart, exploring them on a deep level. The key here is to pay attention to the strength of this quality. Exploring this type of feedback can have great benefits for you as long as you can make sure you aren't taking it all too personally.

In relationships, this can be the cause of fights or disagreements. A partner may give you some feedback in a way that is well-intentioned, but you might get hurt and end up becoming angry instead of appreciating what they said or looking for ways to get better. Remember to keep in mind that you have strong reactions and let them pass or at least calm down before you respond.

- **You can Thrive in the Right Team Environment:** The fact that you can accurately read and empathize with the feelings of other people means that you can thrive in team environments (with the right people). You have a tendency to notice various aspects of decisions that are complex or multifaceted, paying attention to factors that others may not have picked up on. Your heightened imagination gives you insight into various problems that could crop up, helping with prevention of future issues.

  But, when it comes to being or working in group environments, you may be more of an analyzer and advice-giver in these situations rather than an action-taker. You may find that you are a bit too shy or polite to feel comfortable bossing others around or telling them what to do. When combined with people who know how to take action when necessary, you can become unstoppable.

- **Your Creativity is Something to be Celebrated:** Since you notice small details and know how to think in innovative ways, you are highly creative. You may not have realized previously what it was that was different about the way you think, but you've always been able to tell that you think in a different way than others. This allows you talent in areas like writing, music, or painting. You may even find that others marvel at your various talents. This is something to be proud of!

  In addition to these great talents, your creativity also allows you to be a great problem solver, which makes you an amazing partner. Again, understanding your own traits and personality is the most important part about being happy or in a healthy relationship. Once you can recognize and own these traits, you can use them to be even more fulfilled and at peace in your personal life and with other people.

Remember to Trust yourself:

As mentioned in an earlier chapter of this book, learning how to trust your feelings is an important part of thriving as this personality type. You must be in touch with your own feelings so that you can understand why you feel the way you do and what to do about it. A great way to get better at this is to simply practice stopping and noticing what is going on inside of you at any given moment. If you don't already keep a journal, recording these thoughts down in a notebook can be extremely helpful for getting into this habit.

Having intense reactions to situations in life, without understanding why or what you are really feeling, can be overwhelming and lead to anxiety or depression. It's very important that you, as a highly sensitive person, start to realize that there is nothing wrong with this and that you can learn to be perfectly happy this way, even using your powers of observation and intense feeling to have a deeper relationship with your partner. In the next chapter, we will explore more about highly sensitive people in relationships.

CHAPTER 3: UNDERSTANDING A HIGHLY SENSITIVE PARTNER

Relationships tend to be quite complicated, regardless of your personality type. And certain statements about relationships are true for everyone, no matter how they are, such as fighting is not enjoyable. Gestures of appreciation or romance are typically a positive thing, communication is highly valuable and compromising can be highly difficult. But many of these subtleties are noticed only when you are the more sensitive type of partner.

Keep these Factors in Mind about HSP in Relationships:

Whether you are a highly sensitive person in a relationship with someone, or you are someone in a relationship with a highly sensitive person, or you are both sensitive, there are some important things to remember.

- **They Take Relationships Seriously:** Since HSP are so emotionally driven and reactive, they do not typically take relationships in a lighthearted way. They do not typically think of things unless there is some type of emotionally motivation behind it. This could be fear, love, or simple curiosity. Either way, we think about things only when we really feel something about them; otherwise our mind will pass over it. Remember that if a highly sensitive person is involved with you, it's for a reason.

- **HSP are Intuitive:** We have already gone over the point that highly sensitive folks notice subtle cues and nuances in conversation or social situations, but this also relates to your relationship. If the loved one of a HSP is upset, the HSP is definitely going to pick up on it, probably instantly, as we are very sensitive to shifts in mood. Remember that they are noticing changes in your tone, often even over text.

- **Highly Sensitive People have a Hard Time with Conflict:** Getting into arguments with loved ones is not enjoyable for anyone. However, for a highly sensitive person, it is especially negative and uncomfortable. This is due to the fact that they are often undergoing an intense debate inside of them while it is happening. They get stuck between saying what they feel and trying to avoid confrontation.

HSP tend to respond in a more productive way to experiences that are positive, rather than the opposite. Although partners may wish to resolve conflict as they arise, when tensions are high, this can feel difficult or nearly impossible for the HSP. They need a chance to process their emotions first and let things calm down, then come to a solution through supportive talking, not aggression.

- **HSP Must have their Emotions Validated:** Telling a HSP that they are being too sensitive or taking things personally when they don't need to can actually feel very insulting. For a highly sensitive person, it isn't possible to have too many emotions and it can be painful when those are viewed as some kind of weakness. If you tell a HSP to stop being sensitive, they will probably withdraw.

- **They are Easily Bored:** People who are sensitive tend to get a bit restless when it comes to relationships devoid of deep connections and meaningful talks. This doesn't mean that they will easily give up, in fact. It could mean that they are motivated to make more of an effort to start interesting conversations and connect more deeply.

- **They Want their Emotions to be Noticed:** HSP show what they feel, whether it's sadness or happiness. Being with someone who understands and appreciates you is a must, since sensitive individuals cannot help but be expressive. It's just who they are.

- **Make sure Dates include Time for Talking:** The typical HSP's idea of a perfect date will involve some time to talk. While parties can be fun, avoiding over-stimulating environments will be appreciated. Plus, the company is a highly sensitive person's top priority, with details of the date coming in second in importance.

- **They Listen Closely to their Partner's Desires:** Highly sensitive people are intuitive about their mate's desires and have the ability to figure out what they wish for and follow through with it. This applies in love relationships as well as friendships. They care a lot about making their significant other satisfied; and when they aren't, it isn't a good feeling.

- **You don't have to have the Same Personality:** A highly sensitive person does not have to have a partner with the same personality. In fact, relationships between two very different people (as far as sensitivity levels go) can be quite harmonious. The important factor is understanding each other's traits and being able to appreciate them. Don't ever think that just because your partner is highly sensitive, they expect you to be.

Just like any other relationship, a relationship with a highly sensitive person will take work, understanding, and patience.

It's just part of love. However, the more interested you are in your partner's personality, and the more willing you are to work with their inherent traits, and the better off the partnership will be. In fact, if you are open minded enough, you might learn a thing or two from your sensitive significant other.

CHAPTER 4: HABITS THAT SHOW YOU ARE HIGHLY SENSITIVE

Have you noticed that you seem to reflect on life more often than those around you? Are you often preoccupied with wondering what other people are feeling? Do you tend to enjoy environments that are less chaotic and quieter over loud and busy ones? If these apply to you, you are probably a highly sensitive person. Interest, in recent times, toward the trait of introversion has shed some light on traits in people that are more sensitive and prefer less stimulation. Although more research is being done on this subject, and more people are becoming interested, it still seems that very sensitive people are the minority.

But just because this trait is less common, doesn't mean it isn't good. Actually, being a HSP comes along with wonderful benefits. Here are some habits that highly sensitive people display, along with their beneficial features. This list will also give connections between the mental and emotional habits of highly sensitive people and the love relationships they find themselves in.

Do these Habits fit your Personality, and How do they Relate to Love?

- **You Tend to Think with your Heart:** Do you tend to listen to your heart in regards to coming up with solutions or ideas? This is a sure sign that you are highly sensitive, and it is a great quality for relationships. But watch out and make sure you also pay attention to the logical side of things.

  Thinking with your heart is what allows you to be so connected with yourself and your needs. It also lets you see the deepest desires and needs of those close to you, making you a fantastic partner and friend. Knowing how to analyze situations with your heart is great as long as it's balanced out with the whole picture and not just one side of things.

- **You Like to Talk things Through:** A HSP has a need to freely express their emotions and thoughts about every subject. This is necessary in relationships for feeling appreciated and heard by their partner. They enjoy offering support and giving advice, but make sure that you also listen when others try to offer you advice or well-meaning criticism.

  In relationships, you need to feel as though you can come to your partner with anything, and a partner that you need to hide feelings or thoughts from is one that won't last long. If you are in a committed relationship, make sure this aspect is present or you likely will not feel fulfilled with that person and it could lead to resentment.

- **You never Need to Rush:** This is one of the best qualities of highly sensitive people; they like to take their time in life and to enjoy every passing moment. This quality can rub off on others, helping them remember to slow down and notice all of the details of life. Highly sensitive people need to be allowed to express this quality, without feeling rushed by another person.

  If they feel pressured by others, it might add stress to relationships and put trust at risk. This is a highly important factor for compatibility in HSP relationships. When it comes to tense conversations, try to focus on the positive when talking things out, and find ways to compromise so that you are both happy.

- **You, at times, Put up a Tough Front:** People who are highly sensitive may put up a tough front as a way to conceal what they are feeling, because they don't think it will be taken well or understood. In fact, this can cause you to suppress issues, staying mad at a friend without ever revealing why. Perhaps you were hurt by a comment your friend made and want to keep it inside to avoid conflict.

However, in healthy love relationships (and also friendships), it's important to be able to share your concerns openly whether you feel you are being overly sensitive or not. Make sure that when you bring up concerns, or something that made you angry, you do it in a way that doesn't come off as accusatory.

- **You are a Highly Passionate Person:** In areas regarding family members, close friends, or your romantic partner, you are never short of passion and excitement. The exception to this is when you find yourself in situations that you feel you are not being valued or appreciated. Appreciation and enthusiasm from others is important to you, so you should make sure that this is present in your love relationship. Otherwise, you may not be able to flourish at your highest possible potential.

- **You Tend to be Spiritual in your Beliefs:** You have a tendency to believe that things happen not just randomly, but for specific reasons. You believe that the world is working in a way that makes sense, even if you can't always see it at the time. Your ability to see the bigger picture, and patterns of life in retrospect, allows you to take on new situations with a calm composure.

You are likely to try out yoga or meditation, even if it's only once, as a way to expand your mind and body connection. This can be a great way to go deeper with your partner, if they also show an interest in these topics.

- **You Trust the Signals your Body Sends you:** Whenever you are making an important, life-altering decision, such as signing a crucial legal contract, you may notice signals going off inside you. These will tell you whether the decision is good or bad, and you have learned from experience to trust these intuitions. It's important to be with a partner who knows this about you and respects your need to heed these calls.

  Being with someone who laughs or shrugs off these feelings you get will bring you further from your higher self and could lead to issues down the road, both personally and in the relationship.

- **You may put Other People before Yourself:** Sometimes, you get too caught up in what other people need, which can lead you to forget about your own needs. It's important to first know yourself well enough to recognize your needs and wants, and second to be assertive enough to state these with confidence. This all comes down to the level of respect you have for yourself, which will reflect in the relationships you hold.

  In love, you must find a partner who is appreciative, even if it just means that they never forget to say "thank you". These small gestures go a long way for you, and trying to fit with someone who doesn't go along with this could end up being a struggle. Make sure that you assert these needs in order to have healthy relationships with others.

- **You Like to Ask Questions:** You like to understand the world around you, and the people in it, so you ask questions. At times, these questions can be too forward or deep for people, leading to awkwardness. In relationships, it's important to have a partner who also likes to explore ideas with you or will at least give some thought to your curious questions.

  In order to feel fulfilled in life, you should make sure that the people you spend your time with are compatible in this way. You can easily draw inspiration from other curious, passionate people around you, learning from them and becoming a better person as a result.

- **You are a Great Problem Solver:** You are definitely not simple minded. Your multifaceted access to the nuances and emotions within you allow you to think up plenty of creative solutions to all of the issues in life. You enjoy mapping out multiple possible answers to problems and then finding ways to solve them.

  A compatible partner will recognize and appreciate this

trait within you, taking your opinions seriously and considering them fully. The will respect your intuition, as well as all of the thought and feelings you put into coming up with answers to problems. The right partner will hold your intuitions and feelings in high regard, never shrugging them off.

- **You Stand up for What you Know is Right:** Once you get a vision, thought, feeling, or idea, you are not afraid to express it, even if you're the only one with that opinion. This can lead you to feel like you have a hard time relating to others and can be disheartening if you don't have anyone around who recognizes this trait in you and appreciates it or takes it seriously.

  It's important for a highly sensitive person to be with a partner who knows how important it is to you to stay true to your feelings. They will look for ways that they can learn from you in this way. Just make sure that you are also open to your partner's feelings, so that this is mutual and healthy.

- **You Know how to Admit it When you're Wrong:** An HSP is aware of the importance of getting credit for doing things right. Naturally, this means that you have no qualms about admitting it when you've made a mistake. This is a great strength when it comes to relationships, since you aren't interested in wasting time holding onto a wrong opinion stubbornly. Instead, you can move on from conflict swiftly and find your way to creative solutions.

Again, benefiting from your personality type is all about recognizing and using your strengths. The most compatible partner in a love relationship will know your sensitivity, cherish it, and take it seriously, learning from it and appreciating you for these unique traits.

CHAPTER 5: NAVIGATING RELATIONSHIPS AS A HSP

Highly sensitive people are, in a sense, an entirely unique species of human. While some people may constantly seek out or need to have togetherness or be in a relationship, you would rather wait until the right situation comes around than settle for less. This is because you are sensitive to the energies of your partner and tend to absorb what they feel. This can lead to anxiety, overload, or exhaustion when you don't have access to enough space.

Why Some Highly Sensitive People Avoid Partnerships:

An HSP can also be called a super-responder. Your experience of sensory data in a partnership can be compared to feeling things times 100. People who are sensitive in this way might avoid relationships without even being aware that they do it, since they don't want to get engulfed by someone else. They might also feel that coupling up with someone is constricting to their flow of life and need for solitude. Not recognizing and understanding this quality in yourself might lead you to feel lonely. You might crave companionship, while also feeling afraid of it. As soon as you know how to set up healthy boundaries and find ways to work with your preferences, you can find intimate situations to flourish within.

What is Needed for a HSP to Feel Okay in a Partnership?

For the highly sensitive to feel okay in partnerships, the basic idea of a relationship may need some redefinition. This means, at the forefront, knowing how to express your needs for personal time and space. You cannot experience freedom of feelings with someone else until they respect this. The amount of space needed for you, personally, is entirely up to you and depends upon your upbringing, situation and culture.

Everyone has an invisible border or threshold that is needed for a level of comfort to be set. Knowing what yours is, and clearly stating it to others, will help you stay energetically healthy and balanced. This can allow intimate relationships to bloom, even if they were previously suffocating. Possible mates might seem more like drains on your emotions and energy than anything else until you are aware of how to bring up the personal space issue. This may call for the necessity of educating your loved one, communicating that it isn't something personal against them but simply your personality type that makes this necessary.

Practical Tips for Harmonious HSP Relationships:

- **Share your Needs:** This is better stated early on as you get to know someone. Tell them that you are highly sensitive and crave time alone. If the person understands this, it's a good sign. If, however, they pressure you to go against your wishes, it's a sign of disrespect and incompatibility.

- **Make your Sleep Preferences Known:** Most of the time, romantic partners share a bed. However, some sensitive people don't like to do this, regardless of how close they feel to the person. This is not a personal affront; it's just a preference. If you feel more trapped when you share a bed with a person than anything, you should share this. Make sure this is understood and a compromise can be reached.

- **Think of Creative Arrangements for Living Together:** You might be really excited to be in a relationship, until you begin sharing a place. This is a great chance to try out some creative arrangements for living so you feel more comfortable in your place. You need your space, so ask yourself what this looks like, ideally. Would you rather have your own room, or share one?

  Some people prefer to have their own space instead of living with their significant other at all, which is completely fine. Not every couple has to move in together, and you can still have a healthy relationship from separate houses or apartments. Especially for highly sensitive people, having someone always around may not be the ideal situation.

- **Make sure you Take Breaks:** Highly sensitive folks need their time alone to recover from social stimulation, even if it's only brief moments. This can go a long way. Make sure you are always staying cognizant of this and taking a few minutes to regroup when you are in highly stimulating environments.

  A lot of people mistakenly believe that relationships have to look a certain way to be "normal" or healthy, but looking at relationships from a creative perspective can go a long way. As soon as you know yourself well enough to be able to state what you need, freedom emotionally is possible, even with intimate relationships. It should never be a choice between one or the other.

Although you may be particular about the specifics, when it comes to finding a partner or settling down, as a HSP, it's likely that you love being connected with others and appreciate intimacy. The closeness that comes with personal, deep relations is very meaningful to you, even if finding and keeping a partnership is not always so simple. At times, you may wonder if the right love situation is really out there, or if you're being too idealistic. So does this kind of connection exist out there? If it does, how should you go about finding it?

What Makes the Highly Sensitive Great Partners:

They are often romantic, nurturing, idealistic people, which can be great qualities in a partnership. They care on a deep level about others, always willing to lend a hand or a listening ear. They don't do this because they are hoping for something in return, but because they are acutely aware of the needs and feelings of other people on an intense level, often placing themselves in another's position without knowing they are doing it.

The natural warmth, compassion, and empathy of the HSP attracts other people like a magnet, and we are equally attracted to others since we sense their feelings. But this is where the situation can get hard. It's easy to get drawn into others that have deep problems, because we see their pain and want to help. To us, it's similar to seeing someone with a physical injury and trying to ignore that and pretend it isn't there. Sometimes, we don't see these issues until we're already closely involved with someone else and emotionally invested, and it drains our energy and even damages us.

Take Care of Yourself First:

The important thing for highly sensitive people to remember is that regardless of our empathy, compassion, or sensitivity, it's impossible to change others. It's everyone's responsibility to care for themselves, and it is never your job to save someone from their own problems. You should always make sure that you are maintaining balance in your own life and taking care of your own soul. This makes you an even better support system when a friend needs you.

How to do This Effectively as a HSP:

Help yourself first. Since highly sensitive folks are caring naturally and enjoy helping people, it's important to remember not to neglect your own needs. You have to place yourself first, even if it sounds selfish at first glance.

- **Notice the Signs:** Remember that when you get signals of stress, overwhelm, anxiety, or depression, your sensitive inner-self is trying to communicate something to you.

- **Look Within:** The only one who can respond to and fix the issue is you yourself. Never see it as another person's responsibility because they are not you and will not know how to fix the problem adequately, although they may be able to help a bit along the way.

- **Take Time:** You have to know when to take yourself out of unhealthy or stress-inducing situations, allow quiet time and space for yourself, and discover an outside to pour your feelings and creativity into.

The Benefits of Regular Self-Care:

Doing the steps outlined above on a regular basis is a process that will take some time to get into the habit of. The more you do it, the easier it will be to remember to do it. Making sure that you offer yourself this much-needed self-care will provide you with the following benefits:

- **A Higher Self-Esteem:** Doing this will give you a boost to your self-image since it will help you see how crucial it is to help yourself, meaning that you are important and worth time and consideration.

- **Attraction of Healthy People:** When you take the time to care for yourself and feel good about life, you will find yourself attracting like minds who are able to give in relationships instead of just take.

- **A Strong Inner-Focus:** This will help you keep your attention on your personal needs instead of another person's. This will help guard you against being sucked into the problems of others, which can be an energy drain.

- **The Ability to Recognize your Needs:** The more effort you make to truly understand your own needs (creativity, calm, quietness, etc.), the simpler you will find it to turn down what is not necessary. The more comfortable you get with this, the more room you have to accept the right situations into your life, including the right love partner.

How Caring for Yourself Helps you Find a Partner:

This may sound counter-intuitive. After all, isn't finding a partner about focusing on other people? Actually, you will find that it's easier to find a great significant other if you focus on your own interests and needs since you will have a happier outlook, in general. You might find that going outside of your safety zone is helpful to meet new people of a similar mind. Highly sensitive folks tend to hand out where there is art, books, music, writing, or nature-related activity. You will find great relief in finding a social life or love relationship that fits you, rather than trying to bend yourself into an unnatural shape.

How to Tell if you're in a Healthy Situation:

As a HSP, it isn't always easy to tell when you are actually helping someone, or simply wasting your time and energy. Since you get so much out of nurturing others, it can be easy to feel as though draining your own energy is worth it. But remember this; helping other people should leave you feeling braver, smarter, stronger, and healthier. This should make you feel confident and empowered. If the reality is that you feel confused, fearful, weaker, or drained after trying to help, you are not actually helping at all. There are plenty of people out there who will appreciate and respect your empathy without taking it for granted.

Don't make the mistake of believing that these changes will be instantaneous. It will take some effort, but paying attention to the way you feel during various situations in life can help you realize which choices you are making unconsciously. This will then allow you to choose what you wish to have in life, using your emotions as a compass. This could mean you either stay or leave a social event, a career, or a partnership. Don't worry about what other people tell you to do. Take your own needs into consideration and remember to stay ashore.

CHAPTER 6: TIPS FOR HIGHLY SENSITIVE PEOPLE

HSPs have the displeasure of being seen as broken or weak by others. However, intensely feeling has nothing to do with being weak, only being compassionate and fully alive. There shouldn't be any shame related to sharing your true emotions and feelings, and you should never hold back your real self. But anyone who is highly sensitive knows that that is easy to say, but not always easy to do. You get stuck wondering why you seem to get more easily overwhelmed than others, or spend time thinking about events that others forget. It almost seems as though you have thinner skin than others and are less protected. This leads you to try to hide your sensitivity, numb the trait, or ignore it altogether. But since this is a natural part of you, it never works for long, and you are often left frustrated at being different.

Reasons like this make discovering the concept of highly sensitive people revolutionary for those who fit the personality type. You can then see that a lot of others feel different in the same ways that you do. You find out that there is an explanation, after all, for why you have always reacted to stimuli or circumstances differently than the people around you in life. Your nervous system simply processes data more intensely than other people's. This leads you to think and feel deeply and get overstimulated easily. Many revolutionary human beings have shared this trait, such as Steve Jobs and Martin Luther King, which shows that this trait is not a weakness or disadvantage.

The Importance of Knowing How to Handle your Personality:

This is all well and good, unless you don't know how to deal with your own sensitivity and try to push yourself to be more like others. Not taking your sensitivity into account during life will definitely lead to issues that can be prevented ahead of time. While at first you might do a great job utilizing your natural advantages, such as being creative, a great employee, or a devoted partner, when you press yourself past your natural limits, it will lead to negative results and fatigue. You may notice new conditions popping up, serious tension in your muscles, or feeling constantly tired, anxious, or edgy for no discernible reason. If any of this applies to you, read on for how to handle it.

Tips for Thriving as a Highly Sensitive Person:

- **Don't Look Outside yourself for a Fix:** Being sensitive is a trait of your personality, not a mental condition, meaning that there isn't anything bad or wrong about it. You might respond to stress or get anxious quicker than other people, but this does not mean you need professional help. An HSP who becomes a success realizes that there is no inherent brokenness to them. If you find yourself obsessing about finding ways to fix what is "wrong" with you, you're looking in the wrong place.

The real solutions for learning to live in peace with yourself cannot be found outside of you, but have to be discovered yourself. It's only possible to have a truly healthy relationship once this aspect is covered and taken care of; otherwise we can simply feel like a burden to our partner.

- **Remind yourself that you aren't a Fake:** Feeling like an imposter is something that sensitive individuals feel, but it isn't just them that feel it. A lot of people with high achievements notice this fear, but for the HSP, it may just be that much more intense. And this makes perfect sense if you have spent your whole life feeling like a different species than other people and attempting to make yourself fit. This could be hiding your tears during an emotional scene on a movie or being embarrassed that your body takes longer to bounce back from intense exercise than your friends'.

People who are sensitive, yet also successful, know that they are different than up to 85 percent of the population. If you find yourself obsessing about the way you should be and the ways you don't measure up, start realizing that you have your own unique gifts to offer that will stay hidden if you keep trying to be someone you are not.

- **Find people who Get and Appreciate you:** It's important to have people in your life who are kindred and understand your personality, especially since you've always felt alone in your differences. The fact of the matter is, it's a common experience to feel isolated in your own issues and then discover that many others share your experience. The empowerment that comes from realizing this and feeling supported is unlike anything else and can be truly life-transforming.

  One of the best things you can do for yourself is to seek out similar personality types who are succeeding in the ways you wish to so that you can learn from them. The ones who are aware of how to care for their own sensitive ways and also use them as strengths. Successful highly sensitive people relish and appreciate their inner-strengths which are directly related to their sensitive nature. If you don't feel understood or supported, seek out a mentor who can help you.

- **Search for the Good in all Situations:** Our minds are highly effective and powerful lenses of experience that shape our perception by habit. If you believe this world is hostile and dangerous, your mind will seek out confirmation of this. However, if you see it as a friendly place, you will notice that you see more of it. Whatever qualities of life you hone in on, you will see manifested in your daily life. For highly sensitive people, stressful environments can cause nearly unbearable suffering. However, this works both ways; and the better and more positive a situation is, the better you can thrive.

What you think gets directly sent to the nervous system, and it's crucial to recognize negative aspects and know how to let go of them. Ignoring negative aspects will only cause them to become stronger. Try instead to surround yourself with positive people, situations, and thoughts. Making a habit of this will go a long way to making you feel better on a daily basis and relieving your stress.

If you want to enjoy success as an HSP, decide now to view this planet as full of chances to feel happy and bask in a vibe of positivity. This is where your ability to feel things strongly comes in handle, because you can really turn up the happy vibes at will. Whenever you feel jerked around by your circumstances or feelings, remember that your mentality (and the feelings that result) are always generated within you and are thus in your hands. This, if wielded consciously, can be your greatest power.

- **Figure out New Ways to View Old Issues:** Your natural sensitivity comes with a tendency to reflect and see every consequence and angle of a situation. However, the fact that you have access to details in this way leads you to get exhausted or overwhelmed easily when stimulation is constant. For highly sensitive people who don't realize that this happens due to their sensitivity, these could be mistaken as negative traits. But, truthfully, these "flaws" are just your needs being unmet and great gifts to benefit from.

  When you learn to frame your past in a new way and take care of the present respectfully, you will notice a more successful future for yourself. To be successful, you must reframe the old ideas you had about your sensitivity, seeing it in the light of understanding. If you find yourself feeling heavy because of your neglected and super sensitive traits, try to see another perspective. Look at your strengths of vision and intuition.

- **Be Compassionate with Yourself:** Being an HSP means that you have a natural and deep compassion, which can translate to placing the needs of others ahead of your own. This in combination with your tendency to criticize yourself can lead to trouble. You may even berate yourself in a way that you'd be staunchly against berating other people. Try asking yourself next time you feel like talking down on yourself, whether you would treat a close friend this way. You should at least be treating yourself as well as you would treat a friend.

Knowing how to keep this negative self-talk under control is an important element in having true compassion for yourself. However, you should never ignore it. Thinking deeply is a strength you have, so it doesn't make sense to pretend that that power is not there. Instead, regain control by listening to your thoughts from a stance of non-judgment. They might hold something valuable in them, then you can steer them toward thoughts that lead to loving and kinder feelings and sensations within you.

From this new place of understanding, you can make better decisions about self-care and appreciation. This will lead to happier relations with others as well. To be successful as an HSP, you must extend your compassion to yourself as well. Although you may feel a reluctance to do this, feeling selfish, you are not selfish.

- **Construct Boundaries instead of Walls:** Our modern world glorifies pushing on through hard times more than it glorifies the sensitive approach to life. We are all conditioned with thoughts that pain will lead to victory, that the fittest survive, and that life is hardly ever fair. Our admiration goes to people who show tough perseverance through hardships.

As someone who is an HSP, you may notice the temptation to try to get tougher or even freeze up in the face of this pressure. You might end up building protective walls to prevent getting hurt, repress emotions, or even create drama to distract yourself from true pain sources. This could also translate to physical effects, like adding on weight, or walls in a mental sense, or like numbing yourself with drugs or alcohol.

You might also be tempted to collapse these walls simultaneously, absorbing the energy and emotions of other people unconsciously. You may try to avoid these emotions by analyzing everything obsessively, tuning out your intuitive gifts. A successful HSP knows how to be gentle yet strong in their boundaries. If you have a hard time helping yourself before others (a struggle of many sensitive people), learn to practice lovingly declining offers you don't resonate with.

- **Avoid Extreme Emotion Switches by Paying Attention:** You can learn to turn your attention inward to your physical body in order to avoid the pendulum effect of extreme emotions. A lot of sensitive people start suppressing their body's signals, in order to avoid becoming overwhelmed by these sensations or in order to go through their days undisturbed by the distraction of those sensations.

But trying to tune out these natural signals will lead you to swing back and forth between extreme states of feeling. This can be recognized in the phenomenon of being overwhelmed by excitement for some time and then switching to extreme boredom that many highly sensitive people experience. To work with, instead of against, this tendency, you should learn to tune into your body's sensations, accepting that it may not always feel nice, but that it's your body's job to give you guidance.

If you notice that you have a tendency to hide your feelings, commit to begin noticing this. Start paying attention to the signs your body gives you that overstimulation is near. This will allow you to work with differing levels of arousal instead of getting off balance or rocked back and forth by extreme states.

- **Decide for Yourself which Habits of Health Suit you:** As an HSP, you will notice that too much pressing on through exhaustion eventually plays its toll on you. This can mean hours of overtime, working out for too long, followed by a bustling home life, running on low quality food and not enough sleep or resting time. Since most people around you probably live this way, it can be easy to fall into patterns like this, since it seems so normal.

In addition to this, some habits that people claim are healthy are not very good for a nervous system that is more sensitive, like yours. This can mean overly intense fitness workouts that don't allow for enough time to recover, or foods that are sold as health products but actually are full of chemicals or sugar. If you're spending too much time overstimulated with not enough recovery time, you will find yourself getting sick often and feeling constantly tired and overworked.

Focus, instead, on finding healthful habits that feel good *to you*, instead of just believing that they are healthy because they work for other people. If you notice that you have a hard time with general happiness or energy levels, nurture habits that recharge you and work on cutting out draining activities. No matter how much well-meaning advice you receive, listening to your body is the only way to know what is truly right for you as an individual. From this, you can craft the best habits for your well-being and health.

- **Quit Ignoring your Sensitive Traits:** After years and years of being overwhelmed by your surroundings, it can become a habit to shove sensitivity away and try not to think about it. Trying to pretend that you don't care about the sensations you feel constantly, or trying to cut out your intense emotions to stay off of the rollercoaster, or suppressing your feelings to give yourself a break.

This mechanism for protecting yourself may work for fooling your brain. However, it won't ever work for fooling your body. This suppression will leak over into your life, affecting relationships, your job, and your health. The tension will build up higher and higher until you finally decide to stop trying to control this aspect of yourself. As soon as you commit to freeing up that energy, you can flourish, using your gifts of creativity and empathy to their fullest potential. You will then see that your sensitivity is a gift, and never was a curse.

CONCLUSION

Thank you again for buying this book!

I hope this book was able to help you to recognize your personality trait as something positive that can benefit you greatly in life and help you live more fully. Without understanding or recognizing sensitivity in yourself, it's hard to go through life without confusion. You may have noticed that you have always been "different" without understanding why. This book was created with the intention of helping you see the strength in your innate gifts and using those gifts to build and develop stronger love and relationships.

The next step is to work on accepting your personality entirely, finding out what is healthy for you and what isn't. Then, you can communicate all of this to your partner, making sure that they fully understand what your needs and wants are. If you are dating someone who is highly sensitive, I hope that this book helped you to understand the person more.

Finally, if you enjoyed this book, then I'd like to ask you for a favor. Would you be kind enough to leave a review for this book on Amazon? It'd be greatly appreciated!

Thank you and good luck!

Thank you!

Thank you for buying *Empath*. If you enjoyed reading this book, then I'd like to ask you for a favor, **would you be kind enough to leave a review for this book on Amazon? It'd be greatly appreciated!**

All my best wishes,

Josephine T. Lewis

Made in the USA
Lexington, KY
19 February 2019